POLITICAL AGITATORS IN INDIA

POLITICAL AGITATORS IN INDIA

EDITED BY

SURENDRANATH BANERJEA

GYAN

Published by

Gyan Publishing House
5, Ansari Road
Daryaganj, New Delhi-110002
Phone: 011-47034999, 9811692060
E-mail: books@gyanbooks.com

Distribution Network
gyanbooks.com
India, USA, Canada, UK, Australia, France

ISBN: 978-81-212-8955-9 (PB)
First Published, 1907

2nd Impression 2023

Printed at: Gyan Press, Delhi.

POLITICAL AGITATORS IN INDIA

EDITOR: SURENDRANATH BANERJEA

POLITICAL AGITATORS

IN

INDIA

BENGAL.

SECRET.

SURENDRANATH BANERJEA (OF CALCUTTA).

Born about 1848. Educated at Doveton College, Calcutta, from 1856 to 1867. B. A., Calcutta, 1868. Proceeded to England, passed into the Indian Civil Service, and came out to India in 1871. Was posted to Sylhet District. In 1873 he was reported to Government for serious misconduct, the Judges of the High Court holding that he was unfit for the exercise of any judicial powers. A commission was accordingly appointed and 14 charges framed. He was found guilty of "falsehood and of a palpable abuse of his judicial powers" and the Secretary of State directed his removal from the service. (Despatch 31st March 1874.) He was given a compassionate allowance of Rs. 50 a month.

Since then he has been an uncompromising opponent of the system of Government under which he failed. He is the father of anti-British agitation in Bengal, especially among the student community with whom he has great influence. He founded the Ripon College, and it was at a meeting held in this college on 17th July 1905 that the boycott movement was inaugurated in Bengal.

Has edited for many years the *Bengalee* newspaper. Has identified himself with the anti-Partition agitation and devotes most of his energy to keeping it alive. A very good speaker in English, with a good voice and a fluent delivery; but his political writings and speeches, based as they are on personal spite against Government, ring hollow. He shows no more honesty as a public man than he did as a public servant. He is accused by the extremists of want of courage and has long been thrown over by them.

S 05 Cr.

In the anti-Partition agitation he has been supported, particularly this year, by the Hon'ble Babu Bhupendranath Bose; through the latter he was able to prevail upon Mr. Abdul Rasul, Bar.-at-Law, to preside and make a speech. His object in doing so is to show that the feeling against the partition is not confined to Hindus, and to try to get the Mahomedans to join in the agitation.

To this end he has associated with himself from time to time one or two Mahomedan paid agitators. These jackals of the swadeshi lion are sometimes put up at meetings to say things which are too low or too obviously false for Surenderanath to say himself. The following are the principal among them :—

(1) Liakat Husain (of Calcutta).

Is an elderly Mahomedan of the Patna district of no standing, and said to be of immoral character. A paid agitator, used by the Hindus to work up the Mahomedans of Eastern Bengal against the Partition. Also used to lecture on *Swadeshi* in Beadon Square, Calcutta, on Sundays, and paraded the streets with parties of boys. Convicted of sedition and stirring up race hatred (sections 124-A. and 153-A, Indian Penal Code), at Barisal in January 1908; released in 1910, and took part in the anti-partition demonstration in Calcutta in October 1910.

(2) Din Mahomed.

Born about 1850 in Dacca District. By birth a high-caste Brahmin, son of Govinda Chandra Ganguli of Bakarganj District, Eastern Bengal. Poor education. Became a Brahmo Samajist. He is said on one occasion to have shot a calf mistaking it for a boar; he applied for advice on the religious point raised first to the Hindu Pandits, but failing to get satisfaction from them turned to the Mahomedan Maulvis. Was persuaded by them to embrace Islam and took the name of Din Mahomed.

He was first a religious lecturer and anti-kine-killing agitator. After the partition he was made use of as a *swadeshi* lecturer, and in 1907 was being paid Rs. 30 a month by a Calcutta society. Has frequently delivered speeches at meetings presided over by Surendranath.

(3) Abul Kasim (of Calcutta).

Born about 1873. Nephew of Maulvi Abdul Jubber, late Presidency Magistrate, Calcutta. Belongs to Burdwan and has some landed property there. B. A. of Calcutta University. As his uncle refused to help him to become a Deputy Magistrate he became a political agitator. Said to be a good speaker in Bengali.

(4) Dedar Bux.

Born about 1852. A low class Mahomedan of the Hoogly District, son of a Food Inspector in the Commissariat Department. Calls himself a Maulvi but knows no Persian or Urdu.

BHUPENDRANATH BOSE, THE HON. BABU—(OF CALCUTTA).

Born about 1860, son of the late Lal Ratan Bose of Khanakul, Hoogly District. Is a B. A., B. L. and a Fellow of Calcutta University. Resides in Calcutta. Practises as an attorney in the High Court and has a large income from this. Has landed property in Calcutta and *zemindaris* in Gaya and Muzaffarpur Districts. He was President of the Bengal Provincial Conference held at Mymensingh in 1905, and took a leading part in *Swadeshi* and anti-partition meetings in Calcutta during the next few years. He was trusted neither by the people nor by the Government, one day posing as a demagogue and next day conferring with the Lieutenant-Governor at Belvedere. In 1910, although a Member of the Viceroy's Council, he took a leading part along with Surendranath Banerjea and K. K. Mitter in the anti-partition demonstration in Calcutta.

SACHINDRA PRASAD BOSE (OF CALCUTTA).

Born about 1883. Belongs to the Jessore district (Bengal). At the time of the partition he was a student in the 4th year class of the City College. In 1905 he made speeches suggesting that all students should leave their schools unless the Government Circular, issued in that year, against their participation in politics was withdrawn, and he afterwards organised the "Anti-Circular Society" in the same connection. In 1906 and 1907 he visited many places in both Bengals supporting the boycott in strong language and organising Volunteer societies. In December 1908 Sachindra was staying at K. K. Mitter's house, and was one of his active lieutenants in organising the *Anusilan Samiti* of Calcutta, of which he was reported to be the "Inspector of Branches."

He was deported in December 1908, his chief importance being that he was K. K. Mitter's lieutenant. Otherwise he is a person of little consequence.

SHYAM SUNDAR CHAKRAVARTY (OF CALCUTTA).

Born about 1870 at Bharenga, Pabna, Bengal. He was known as an agitator before the Partition. He numbered among his friends Arabindo Ghose, P. Mitter (Bar.-at-Law and supporter of the physical force party, lately deceased), B. C. Pal, and Brahmobandhab Upadhyaya (editor of the revolutionary *Sandhya*, who died while on bail under trial for sedition). Shyam Sundar in his early days devoted his attention to strikes and labour troubles, and again in July and August 1906 he was busy encouraging the strikers in the E. I. R. strikes. In 1907 and 1908 he attended numerous extremist meetings, often in the company of Arabindo Ghose.

In 1905 he was Sub-Editor of the *Sandhya*, and at the end of 1906 he left it for Arabindo Ghose's paper the *Bande Mataram*. He was one of the directors of this paper and second only to Arabindo Ghose in its management.

He was deported in December 1908.

S 05 Cr.

BHUPENDRANATH DUTT (OF CALCUTTA).

Born about 1884 at Calcutta. Brother of the late Swami Vivekananda of the Ram Krishna Mission. Said to be of good education, but failed in the B. A. examination. Was editor of the *Jugantar*, and as such was convicted on the 24th July 1907 and sentenced to one year's rigorous imprisonment. He was in close touch with Barin Ghose and the other members of the Alipore bomb conspiracy who used to meet at the *Jugantar* mess. On his release in June 1908 he concealed himself for some time at the Belur Math (a temple of the Ram Krishna Mission near Calcutta). Shortly after he left for America and arrived in New York in the autumn of 1908. He is believed to be still in America.

Keeping rather in the background, he was probably one of the most dangerous leaders of the revolution in Bengal, and his relationship to Swami Vivekananda gave him a sort of religious prestige with the more fanatical members.

ARABINDO AKROYD GHOSE (OF CALCUTTA).

Born about 1872, went to England at the age of 7; educated at St. Paul's School, London, and King's College, Cambridge. Passed into the Indian Civil Service in 1890 but failed in the riding examination. His failure to qualify appears to have turned him against Government.

Came out to India and was appointed professor in the Gaekwar's College, Baroda, in 1893. When the anti-Government agitation in Bengal began to take shape he gave up his post in Baroda and came to Bengal to take service under the National Council of Education at a much lower rate of pay.

Was practically editor of the *Bande Mataram* newspaper, and wrote most of its leading articles on the most extreme lines. Was prosecuted for sedition in August 1907, but his responsibility as editor could not be proved chiefly owing to the refusal of B. C. Pal to give evidence of the fact. In May 1908 his deportation was proposed by the Government of Bengal but negatived by the Government of India.

The garden at Muraripookar, Maniktolla, in which the Alipore bomb conspiracy was centred was the joint property of himself and his brothers, and the head of the anarchist gang, Barindra Kumar Ghose, was one of them. A few days after the Muzaffarpur outrage, 30th April 1908, and the discovery of bombs and the arrest of most of the gang in the Maniktolla garden, Arabindo was arrested and tried along with them. He was acquitted in May 1909 and went to stay at 6, College Square, the house of K. K. Mitter. After his acquittal he gave out that he had received in jail a special message from Sri Krishna to free the country. He started a new weekly paper in English called the *Karmayogin* to expound the doctrines of revolution by violence under the guise of religion, thus continuing the policy of the *Yugantar*. In connection with a seditious article published in this paper on the 25th December 1909 a warrant was issued a month or two later for his arrest. He had been for some time in retirement, and the warrant could not be executed as he had absconded. He was afterwards found to be living in Pondicherry where he still is. The printer of the article referred to was convicted and sentenced to 6 months' imprisonment, but acquitted in appeal by Holmwood and Fletcher, JJ.

The English style of Arabindo Ghose's articles in the *Bande Mataram* was admirable, and he has composed some good poetry in the same language. He is much more a poet and mystic than a man of action. There can be no doubt that he was fully cognisant of the Maniktolla bomb conspiracy and approved of the programme of the conspirators.

MOTI LAL GHOSE (OF CALCUTTA).

Born about 1855. Son of Hari Narayan Ghose of Magura, District Jessore. The Ghose family established a Bazar there which they called, after their mother, the Amrita Bazar, and an elder brother of Moti Lal named Sisir Kumar started the *Amrita Bazar Patrika* (Patrika means newspaper) first as a weekly. Moti Lal Ghose is now the editor of this paper which appears daily in English. He has no University qualifications and received his education at home.

The *Amrita Bazar Patrika* is the great rival of the *Bengalee*, and caters for the same class of readers. For years Moti Lal Ghose and Surendranath Banerjea were not on speaking terms on this account. While they are both anti-Government, their selfish rivalry generally prevents their agreement on points of public policy.

Moti Lal Ghose has not the same personal grievance against Government that Surendaranath has, and does not aspire to be a leader of the mob. His attacks on Government are perhaps on this account more open than Surendranath's and probably more honest. The *Amrita Bazar Patrika* has the saving grace of a kind of caustic humour, of which the *Bengalee* is unfortunately devoid.

MONORANJAN GUHA (OF GIRIDIH, BENGAL).

Born about 1858 at Banaripara, Bakarganj, Eastern Bengal. Owner of mica mines at Giridih, Bengal, and well to do.

He was a prominent anti-partition agitator in 1905 and 1906 at Barisal, and afterwards in Calcutta and the vicinity. He was connected with the seditious *Navasakti* newspaper, was a financial supporter of the Maniktolla anarchist gang, and was frequently consulted by the head of the gang, Barindra Ghose, at the *Navasakti* office.

He was deported in December 1908 ; his case aroused comparatively little comment and since his release in February 1910 he has not come to notice much.

S-05 Cr.

GISPATI ROY CHAUDHARI KABYATIRTHA (OF HOWRAH).

Born about 1872 at Taki, 24-Parganas. Came to notice as an agitator after the Partition. Editor of the scurrilous paper the *Howrah Hitaishi*, and a paid agitator. He made several speeches in praise of convicted seditionaries in 1907 and 1908, and paid frequent visits to the seats of disaffection in both Bengals. Khudiram Bose, the Muzaffarpur assassin, mentioned Gispati as one of the persons whose speeches had made him resolve to die for his country.

Gispati narrowly escaped deportation in 1908. After this he was quiet for a time, but is again taking a prominent part in agitation. His paper, however, has been unable to survive the Press Act. There can be no doubt of his thorough disloyalty and of the pernicious character of his speeches, but otherwise he is a person of minor importance.

KRISHNA KUMAR MITTER (OF CALCUTTA).

Born about 1853 at Tangail, Mymensigh, Eastern Bengal. A Brahmo by religion. Resides at 6, College Square, Calcutta. Editor of the *Sanjibani*, a Bengali weekly, which before the partition had considerable influence in Eastern Bengal. Has always posed as a constitutional agitator. Took a leading part in the anti-partition agitation, and was one of the three leaders who joined the meeting held on the 17th July 1905 at the Ripon College at which it was decided to boycott British goods.

During the next year or two he addressed numerous *swadeshi* meetings strongly supporting the boycott. He was specially conspicuous in working up the *National Volunteer* movement; he and Monoranjan Guha were the founders and organisers of the *Brati Samiti* in Calcutta. In December 1908 he was closely connected with the *Anusilan Samiti* of Calcutta, and his house, at which Sachindra Prasad Bose and Sarojini Ghose (the sister of Arabindo) then resided, was believed to be the real headquarters of this Samiti.

Deported in December 1908, and released in February 1910. His deportation and that of Aswini Kumar Dutt were those which gave rise to the greatest amount of adverse criticism in Bengal. Nobody cared much about the others.

His son Sukumar, who lives in the same house, has been known for some time as a dangerous character, especially owing to his connection with the volunteer movement. The scheme of Virendranath Chattopadhyaya of Paris to import arms for revolutionary purposes into India *viâ* Chandernagore, which came to light in July 1910, was intended to be worked through Sukumar. Virendranath's letter on the subject indicated that Sukumar had already been in communication with him regarding the importation of arms.

K. K. Mitter's daughter, Kumudini, edits a Bengali monthly magazine the *Suprabhat* which was started in July 1907. She advised the young men of Bengal to give up their lives for the country, and her magazine contains many quasi-religious articles and poems advocating and belauding anarchism and assassination on the lines inaugurated by the notorious *Jugantar*, and followed later by Arabindo Ghose in his writings, and by the anarchists of Maniktolla in practice. After the deportation of her father the magazine became less outspokenly revolutionary, and of late its tone has improved still further in consequence perhaps of the Press Act.

Kumidini is one of a trio of three young Bengali ladies—the others being Sarojini Ghose, sister of Arabindo, and Mrinalini Chatterji, sister of Virendranath Chattopadhyaya (or Chatterji) the Paris revolutionary—who have bound themselves together by a vow not to marry in order to devote themselves to the service of their country.

SUBODH CHANDRA MULLICK (OF CALCUTTA).

Born about 1870 ; of good family. Nephew of Mr. M. N. Mullick, Bar.-at-Law, who once stood for Parliament for Hanover Square, London. Educated amongst other places at Cambridge. After the Partition of Bengal he took a prominent part in the agitation against it and later joined the extremists. His importance lay in his being their main financial support. He is believed to have given a lakh of rupees to the National College, which earned for him from the extremists the title of 'Raja.' Subodh Mullick was practically the sole proprietor of the "Bande Mataram Company, Limited," and, as such, financed Arabindo Ghose's paper of the same name. It was evidently intended to propagate sedition as, at one of the searches in Calcutta, a written legal opinion was found on the question how far the shareholders would be responsible for fines if the printer was convicted of sedition.

He was connected with the Alipore bomb conspiracy. Arabindo Ghose was his friend and used to reside at his house, and it was through Arabindo Ghose's brother, Barindra, the head of the gang, that Subodh subscribed to the funds of the *Jugantar*. The fact of his having so subscribed was proved by accounts which were found.

Subodh Mullick was deported in December 1908. His case aroused very little comment considering his wealth and status. Since his release he has been very quiet.

BEPIN CHANDRA PAL (OF CALCUTTA).

Born about 1860. Native of Sylhet. Son of a pleader and petty zemindar. Educated in Sylhet and Calcutta, where he failed in the F. A. Examination. For a time schoolmaster in Sylhet and said to drink heavily. Then joined the Brahmo Samaj and became a Temperance lecturer.

In 1903 visited England and lectured on Brahmoism and Temperance.

In 1904 returned to India and started the *New India* paper which was at first moderate but gradually became seditious. When it failed, he joined the staff of Arabindo Ghose's *Bande Mataram.*

In 1905 and 1906 he addressed numerous boycott meetings, at which he made inflammatory speeches, in Calcutta and throughout Bengal and Eastern Bengal. He continued this proceeding in 1907, extending the sphere of his operations in February to Allahabad and Benares, and in April to the Madras Presidency through which he toured for nearly two months delivering seditious speeches at many of the principal towns.

About this time he was offered a travelling lectureship of Rs. 1,000 a year by Shyamji Krishnavarma of the "Indian Sociologist" in consideration of his delivering 45 lectures a year, 5 in each of 9 principal cities in India, and publishing them in book form. He accepted the offer but the tour did not take place as in September 1907 he was sentenced to six months' imprisonment for refusing to give evidence in the prosecution of Arabindo Ghose for sedition.

On his release in March 1908 he had a great ovation at Howrah station and afterwards went on a lecturing tour in Eastern Bengal, everywhere working up the agitation and encouraging the "volunteers" to resist authority.

At the end of August 1908 he left for England. On his way he saw Shyamji Krishnavarma in Paris and disagreed with him as to his methods; he was afterwards denounced by Shyamji as a traitor, and publicly accused of having accepted Rs. 500 (the first moiety of the lectureship above mentioned) under false pretences.

In England B. C. Pal delivered a number of seditious speeches in London and Cambridge and edited the "Swaraj" Magazine, one issue of which was held by the Bombay Courts to be seditious. The Bombay Agent Modak was convicted under section 124-A, I. P. C., for publishing it. The Magazine then came to an end.

Till the spring of 1909 he was associated with Savarkar and the other revolutionaries in London, and Virendranath Chattopadhyaya was his Sub-Editor on the Magazine. About the middle of 1909 he began to withdraw from the front rank of the revolutionaries, but he kept in touch with them through his son Niranjan Pal who is still a close associate of the leaders in London and Paris.

B. C. Pal is a low type of demagogue; he is, however, a good speaker and knows how to suit his language to his audience. He is equally at home informing an Eastern Bengal meeting that the time has come to sacrifice 100 white goats to *Kali*, or expounding the principles of nationalism and patriotism and the Oriential doctrine of non-resistance to a London audience.

A. RASUL (OF CALCUTTA).

Born about 1870. Educated in England; M. A. of Oxford and Bar.-at-Law. Married an English lady while studying in England. Has some land in Eastern Bengal and practises as a Barrister in Calcutta. He is said to be assisted in his professional work by the Hon'ble Babu Bhupendranath Bose. Although a Mahomedan he has taken part for the last year or two in the *swadeshi* and anti-Partition agitation, being brought forward and encouraged by Surendranath Banerjea and the other Hindu leaders in order to show that they have Mahomedan support. Presided at the anti-Partition demonstration in Calcutta in October 1910.

BOMBAY.

MORESHWAR GOPAL DESHMUKH (OF GIRGAUM, BOMBAY).

Born about 1856. Chitpawan Brahmin. Son of Sirdar Rao Bahadur G. H. Deshmukh, an Inam Commissioner. Has a brother, L. G. Deshmukh, in the Provincial Civil Service, Bombay. Is a B. A., B. Sc., and M. D., of Bombay University. Was Assistant Chemical Analyser to Bombay Government from 1879-92 when he resigned. An orthodox Hindu of good private character. No orator, and seldom addresses meetings or writes to newspapers. A thorough Nationalist of Extremist views. Circumstances connected with his resignation apparently turned him against Government, and from 1892 he joined the Congress and gradually became more extreme in his conduct and asssociates. He was a friend of B. G. Tilak, and accompanied him on a visit to Sholapur in 1908. Deshmukh remains generally behind the scenes ; many suspicious matters suggesting his connection with anarchism have come to notice from time to time in the last year or two, but nothing very definite has yet been brought home to him.

GANGADHAR BALKRISHNA DESHPANDE (OF BELGAUM).

Born about 1869. Deshasth Brahmin by caste. Belongs to Belgaum. Is a B. A. and LL. B., and has a small practice as a lawyer. Has landed property and a house in his native village of Hadli ; income about Rs. 7,000 a year. Has a good position in Hindu society. The leading Extremist agitator of Belgaum. Friend and admirer of B. G. Tilak. Has taken a prominent part in the swadeshi agitation and the Shivaji celebrations. He is strongly suspected of having been concerned in the Kolhapur conspiracy to murder Colonel Ferris in April 1908. In June 1908 Deshpande was reported to be the head of a society in Belgaum called the " Gupta Mandali " (Secret Society) which was apparently in favour of assassination, as a garlanded photograph of the Chapekar Brothers (who committed the Poona murders in 1897) was hung up in the hall of the National School with which this society was connected. Deshpande is apparently on bad terms with the Kolhapur Durbar and police, and in 1910 gave to the Belgaum police information of an attempt made by a Kolhapur man to foist a book of explosives upon him in order to get him into trouble. There is no doubt that he is a thorough extremist, and he was in all probability concerned in the 1908 conspiracy; he has lately withdrawn somewhat from active sedition and his account of the 1910 case seems on the whole to be correct.

S. 05 Cr.

GOPAL KRISHNA GOKHALE (OF POONA), THE HONOURABLE MR.

Very little is known of his early history; he is a Brahmin of the Poona side and for many years he has been a competitor with Tilak for popularity as a political leader in the Deccan. It is said that this is one of his chief reasons for coming forward as a Moderate, and his enemies in the Extremist camp do not hesitate to ascribe to him the institution of proceedings against Tilak, and the failure of their efforts to have his conviction set aside.

Mr. Gokhale is mentioned here as he is the founder of the "Servants of India Society" which he started at Poona in June 1905. In the first printed prospectus one of the objects of the Society was said to be "to train men for the work of political education and agitation, and to promote by all constitutional means the national interests of the Indian people," but this was revised in 1907 on more moderate lines to read, "to train man to devote themselves to the service of India as national missionaries, and to promote by all constitutional means the national interests of the Indian people." This change is an indication of Mr. Gokhale's move in the "moderate" direction, corresponding to Tilak's progress in aggressive extremism.

Mr. Gokhale's own description of the political creed of the Society, taken from the same prospectus, is ingeniously worded as follows:—"The members frankly accept the British connection as ordained in the inscrutable dispensation of Providence for India's good. Self-Government on the lines of English colonies is their goal. This goal they recognise cannot be attained without years of earnest and patient work and sacrifices worthy of the cause."

The Society is in some ways an imitation of the Society of Jesus, requiring as it does implicit obedience to the head. In the first set of rules printed, rule 5 read as follows :—" Every member, on admission, shall be under a vow of absolute obedience to the First Member for five years, " while in the second set, printed before the Society was a year old, the corresponding rule read :—" Every member, on admission, shall undergo a special training for a period of five years," and rule 10 received the amplification that every member during the time he is under training " shall place himself under the entire guidance and control of the First Member." There is not very much difference between the two in practice, and the First Member, Mr. Gokhale, keeps all the control in his hands.

The key to Mr. Gokhale's policy will be found in the constitution of this Society; he accepts the fact of British supremacy "as ordained in the inscrutable dispensation of Providence," but he does not desire its continuance.

RAGHUNATH PANDURANG KARANDIKAR (OF SATARA).

Born about 1857 at Pandharpur, a place of considerable sanctity in the Sholapur District (Bombay). Educated in Satara High School and passed the matriculation of the Bombay University and the District and High Court Pleaders' Examinations. Owns land in Satara and Sholapur districts. Served as a subordinate judge in the 80's. Then practised as a pleader in Nagpur. Returned to Satara where he is one of the leading pleaders. Annual income about Rs. 10,000. He is very well-mannered, and popular in Satara with all classes, especially the extremists, and is familiarly known as "Dada Saheb." He is simple in his habits and does not as a rule wear English clothes. He is one of B. G. Tilak's greatest friends, and as such is also a friend of W. S. Khare of Nasik and G. S. Khaparde of Amraoti. These four form the "Old Guard" of Extremism on the West of India. Karandikar is a thorough extremist who would gladly have the English turned out of India, but does not believe in violent methods which have no chance of success.

When Tilak was arrested in 1908, Karandikar was the first to go off to see him in jail to arrange for his defence, and when he was convicted Karandikar left for England at the beginning of October 1908 to assist with the appeal to the Privy Council. While in London he attended extremist meetings and was much in the society of leading agitators, but he was never known to speak in public and his presence at the India House was not reported. Karandikar has twice attempted, unsuccessfully, to get into the Provincial Council. While in England he succeeded in making the friendship of the Hon'ble Mr. Gokhale and there are other indications of his taking a more moderate line than he used to do.

NARSINH CHINTAMAN KELKAR (OF POONA).

Born about 1872 in Ratnagiri district. Konkanasth Brahmin by caste. Is a B. A., LL. B. Editor of the *Mahratta* newspaper (salary Rs. 100 a month) and occasionally practises as a pleader.

Kelkar's father was a Mamlatdar, and after retirement private *Karbhari* in Miraj (Senior) State. In 1891 Kelkar passed as B. A. from the Deccan College, and in 1894 passed the LL. B., and went to practise in Satara District. Shortly after he went to Poona and obtained a post on Rs. 100 a month as teacher in B. G. Tilak's law classes there. Assisted Tilak as Editor of the *Mahratta* and afterwards became the declared editor.

Kelkar has been engaged in political agitation since 1895, and the paper has always been conducted on extremist lines. Kelkar, however, is more moderate than his chief, and the paper has always escaped a prosecution under the Indian Penal Code. In the issue for 26th July 1908 he published an article on the Tilak case on account of which he was found guilty of contempt of court by the High Court on the 29th September 1908, and sentenced to pay a fine of Rs. 1,000 and to imprisonment for 14 days or until he apologised. He submitted an apology and was released on October 13th. For his "want of firmness" in this matter he was thrown over by the Poona extremists and given leave as editor of the *Mahratta*. He has since, however, been restored to his former post.

The refusal of the Bombay Government to allow him to stand for the Bombay Legislative Council gave rise to a good deal of comment at the time.

KRISHNAJI PRABHAKAR KHADILKAR (OF POONA).

Born about 1871. Chitpawan Brahmin. Son of a landed proprietor of Sangli State, where his elder brother is in State Service. First came to notice in the Shivaji celebrations at Poona in 1899, and in the reception given the same year to the Natu brothers (implicated in the Poona murders of 1897) on their release. Was connected even then with B. G. Tilak's paper the *Kesari*, and has been editor of it since Tilak's conviction. It is very generally believed that Khadilkar was the writer of the articles for which Tilak as editor accepted responsibility and was convicted. Khadilkar has been all along a zealous follower of Tilak, and a fomenter of sedition in Poona and the neighbourhood. Ideas which afterwards bore fruit in Bengal appear to have seen the light first in this much abler *coterie* in Poona, for, as early as September 1905 we find Khadilkar lecturing on the 'Bhagwat Gita , with N. C. Kelkar presiding, and also on 'Animal Sacrifice' with B. G. Tilak in the chair. The lesson he took from the *Gita* was "not to despair of success but to leave everything to God," and on the Hindu doctrine of sacrifice he advised that "as many human lives as would appease the God of Independence be sacrificed for the political regeneration of India." These are the principles which the Bengali revolutionaries borrowed, developed, and applied—prematurely as the Poona extremists thought.

Khadilkar is the author of some objectionable dramas including "Kichak Vadh" (The murder of Kichak), a play based on the *Purans* but believed to be intended to have an allegorical application to the state of India when it was written, Kichak, who was murdered for his sins, being Lord Curzon.

WAMAN SAKHARAM KHARE (OF NASIK).

Born about 1865. A Chitpawan (Konkanasth) Brahmin of Nasik, B. A., LL. B. Owns a little land, and had a good practice as a pleader worth about Rs. 500 a month. Khare was educated at the Nasik High School, and Elphinstone College, Bombay (B. A., 1890). Became LL. B. in 1893 and started practice in Nasik. Has been an agitator since 1895, at first of a mild type. In 1905 he began to become a leading extremist in connection with the Shivaji celebrations. Towards the end he became so violent that the local moderates said he had lost his head over political matters. He is the father of sedition in Nasik, and the teacher of the Savarkar family who carried his lessons into practice in the Nasik conspiracy.

In 1909 proceedings were taken against him under section 108 C. P. C., on account of his seditious speeches and an order was passed binding him over under section 115, C. P. C. This order was upheld by the Bombay High Court. His *sanad* as a pleader was also withdrawn by the High Court, and his suspension was ordered to last so long as he was bound over.

On this he became a *sanyasi* and declared that he would follow a religious life until the end of the period for which he had given security. In this character he wandered about in the Deccan and made his headquarters at a place in the Poona district. He was last heard of in September 1910 as an inmate of the lunatic asylum at Dharwar.

SHIVRAM MAHADEV PARANJPE (OF POONA).

Born about 1865. Konkanasth Brahmin of Mahad in Kolaba District. M. A. of Bombay University.

His importance lies in his having been editor of the Marathi paper the *Kal* which has been for years a good second to the *Kesari* in seditious writing. It was started in 1898, a year after the Poona murders, and its tone was so bad that the editor was warned in 1899. The question of prosecuting the paper was considered in respect of various articles which appeared in 1899, 1900, 1904, 1905 (two occasions) and 1907 (three occasions) but each time the matter was dropped, sometimes because the law officers were doubtful, twice (in 1904) because the Government of India refused to sanction the prosecution, and once (1907) because the Local Government was able to show that the proposal of the Government of India to prosecute was inexpedient.

Paranjpe was convicted of sedition in the Bombay High Court on the 8th July 1908 and sentenced to 19 months' rigorous imprisonment.

The paper came to an end in 1910 through the operation of the Press Act.

THE SAVARKAR FAMILY (OF NASIK).

The family consists of three brothers:—

Ganesh	Damodar	Savarkar	born about	1880.
Vinayak	„	„	„	1883.
Narayan	„	„	„	(1887?)

They are Konkanasth Brahmins of no social status, sons of a small landowner and money-lender of Bhajur in the Nasik district. Ganesh studied up to the Matriculation standard. Vinayak obtained the B. A. degree from the Fergusson College, Poona.

The two elder brothers, Ganesh and Vinayak, were both prominent agitators since 1905 under the guidance of W. S. Khare. They were leaders of the *Mitra Mela*, an association started in connection with the Ganpati celebrations about 1899, and Ganesh personally supervised the teaching of drill, physical exercises and fencing to the Nasik youths. Vinayak prepared a 'Life of Mazzini' in 1905-06, and after his departure for England in June 1906 Ganesh was left to supervise its printing and publication.

Ganesh was convicted at Nasik and sentenced to transportation for life for sedition on June 9th, 1909, and his brother Vinayak, now head of the secret society in England, instigated, in revenge for this, the murder of Sir William Curzon-Wyllie on 1st July 1909. The sentence passed on G. D. Savarkar was confirmed by the High Court of Bombay on November 18th, 1909, and this was followed by the second act of vengeance, also apparently instigated by Vinayak, the murder of Mr. Jackson at Nasik on December 1st, 1909.

Some time before this, information had been received that the third brother, Narayan, was following in the same footsteps. When two bombs were thrown at the carriage of His Excellency the Viceroy at Ahmedabad on November 13th, 1909, enquiries were made as to Narayan's whereabouts, and as his explanation was not satisfactory, he was paraded for identification along with a number of other youths before Mr. Barrow, Commissioner, Northern Division, who rejected all except Narayan and one other, finally fixing on the other who turned out to be a police recruit. Narayan's photograph was afterwards shown to Lady Minto, who was satisfied that he was not the boy who threw the bombs.

It is unnecessary to refer in further detail to Vinayak Savarkar's escape at Marseilles and the international question to which it gave rise, or to the conspiracy case in which he is now under trial in Bombay.

BAL (BALWANT) GANGADHAR TILAK (OF POONA).

Born about 1856. Chitpawan Brahmin of the Ratnagiri District. B. A., LL. B. Proprietor of the *Mahratta* (English weekly) and *Kesari* (Marathi weekly) newspapers of Poona. His father was a Government servant, and when he died in 1872 was Assistant Deputy Educational Inspector. B. G. Tilak took the B. A. degree with honours from the Deccan College, Poona, in 1875, and obtained the LL. B. in Bombay in 1879. Along with two others he opened the New English School in Poona on the 2nd January 1880, and shortly after started the newspapers. In 1882 Tilak and Agarkar, as editors and publishers of these two papers, were tried in the Bombay High Court for defamation contained in comments on a Kolhapur political case and sentenced to 3 months' imprisonment each in each of two cases, the sentences to run concurrently. In 1884 Tilak started the Deccan Educational Society, which in 1885 opened its own college called the Fergusson College after the Governor of Bombay. In 1890 Tilak left this society. He also obtained about this time sole control of the *Kesari* and the *Mahratta.*

In the agitation against the "Age of Consent" Bill he made a bid for popularity and became the leader of the 'Extreme' party, or 'Orthodox' as it then was. From that time onwards he was a persistent opponent of Government, his policy being to obtain Self-Government by any means possible, favouring even rebellion if it had any chance of success. He is said, however, to have been against the Bengal outrages as he considered a resort to violence at that time premature. His influence in the Deccan and the whole Presidency was very great, and a well-informed Poona missionary, writing about the Punjab deportations of 1907 and a suggestion that Tilak should be similarly treated, expressed the opinion that no Government would dare to arrest him. B. G. Tilak was convicted of sedition in the Bombay High Court on the 22nd July 1908 and sentenced to 6 years' transportation, which was afterwards commuted by Government to simple imprisonment.

He was by far the most important seditionary on the Bombay side, and his influence was felt all over India. He owed his position to his great ability and strength of character, and his patriotism does not seem to have been based on a private grudge against Government, as is the case with some of the leading Bengali agitators, all of whom he surpassed in intellect, courage and determination.

Leave to appeal to the Privy Council against his conviction was refused by the Bombay High Court. The Privy Council, however, granted special leave to appeal, and in the end the appeal was heard and rejected. Tilak is confined in Mandalay.

CENTRAL PROVINCES.

GANESH SRIKRISHNA KHAPARDE (OF AMRAOTI).

Born about 1857. Brahmin of humble origin, whose ancestors came from Khaparda, a village in Akola District. His father was a clerk in one of the Hyderabad Contingent Cavalry Messes, and accompanied the regiment to Delhi during the mutiny. He then obtained a civil appointment in Berar and rose to the rank of Extra Assistant Commissioner. He was an able but most unscrupulous magistrate and died a rich man, and the proprietor of houses and lands, in 1893.

G. S. Khaparde matriculated at the Elphinstone College, Bombay, in 1878. He became a B.A., and was appointed Fellow of Sanskrit and English by the Bombay University. In 1885 he took the LL. B. Was appointed direct as Extra Assistant Commissioner in Berar, but failing to obtain the promotion he expected to Assistant Commissioner, he resigned after three years and started as a pleader. At his best he is said to have made about Rs. 4,000 a month.

From about 1890 he became a popular leader, and in 1907 he was Vice-President of Amraoti Municipality and of the District Board, having served on them continuously for 17 years.

His personal intimacy with Tilak dates back to 1897, when Khaparde's son was married to the daughter of Sirdar Baba Maharaj, of Poona, a great friend of Tilak. Before his death the Sirdar appointed Tilak and Khaparde, with others, trustees of his estate; the trustees quarrelled with the widow, Tai Maharaj, and out of this arose the famous Tai Maharaj adoption case. (Tilak was convicted of perjury, in connection with it, by the special Magistrate, and this was confirmed and the sentence reduced by the Sessions Judge of Poona, but the High Court of Bombay acquitted him.)

The idea of boycotting British goods seems to have originated with G. S. Khaparde, for it is on record that he convened a meeting for this purpose as early as 1896.

In 1897 the National Congress met at Amraoti, and Khaparde was President of the reception committee. Throughout the following years he became more and more prominent as an agitator, and his influence throughout the West of India was only second to Tilak's and probably exceeded it in Berar.

Khaparde has been mixed up in many dangerous matters. He is known to have been in correspondence with some of the principal persons concerned in the Poona murders of 1897, and one of the actual murderers, the elder Chapekar, is known to have visited Khaparde, disguised as a ballad singer, a short time before the murders.

Again about the time of the Royal visit to Hyderabad a Nepalese named Rudra Narayan Partab Jung was arrested in suspicious circumstances at Bolarum, but escaped and came straight to Amraoti, across country, disguised as a mendicant. He was found to have a *kukri* and a sharp dagger, and was prosecuted under the Arms Act. On his conviction one of Khaparde's men collected money and paid his fine.

In 1908 one of the principal accused in the Maniktolla Garden bomb case said that he had visited Khaparde at Amraoti to tell him that the revolutionary party in Bengal were prepared to make bombs, and to ask for the subscriptions which Khaparde had promised. He also said that Khaparde had sent B. H. Kane (a youth belonging to Nagpur who was finally acquitted in the Alipore case) to Calcutta to learn the manufacture of bombs.

In August 1908 Khaparde went to England in connection with Tilak's appeal. There he associated with the leading extremists, and the prospectus of B. C. Pal's seditious *Swaraj* magazine was signed by Khaparde and Pal jointly. Khaparde took the chair at one of the India House Sunday meetings on October 11th, 1908, and in his speech described *Bande Mataram* as "the war cry of every true Indian."

After the assassination of Sir William Curzon-Wyllie (1st July 1909) a correspondent reported that in conversation Savarkar said that Khaparde was a sympathiser with such deeds. "Khaparde came to B. C. Pal's house the other day and said that still there was work to be done; one assassination was not sufficient."

In London Khaparde is said to have spent his money on drink and women, and this year (1910) he wrote out to his friends in India for money to enable him to return. Some money was sent, and he has since returned to Amraoti having first sailed direct to Rangoon and visited Tilak in jail at Mandalay.

ACHUYT BALWANT KOLHATKAR (OF NAGPUR).

Born about 1875. Brahmin by caste ; son of a retired Extra Assistant Commissioner of the Central Provinces, but adopted by his uncle and brought up at Poona. Educated at the Bombay High School; B. A. of Bombay University, and LL. B. Practised as a pleader at Nagpur, but was not very successful. Edited the *Desha Sewak*. Became a prominent seditious agitator in Nagpur from 1907. Convicted on 13th December 1908 and sentenced to 2½ years' rigorous imprisonment (reduced on appeal to 15 months) as editor of the *Desha Sewak*, on account of seditious articles which appeared in the paper purporting to be translations of speeches delivered by Arabindo Ghose. His case caused some stir, as he alleged ill-treatment in jail, and complained that while being taken from one jail to another he was compelled to march in irons through the streets of Nagpur.

S. 05 Cr.

BALKRISHNA SHEORAM MUNJE (OF NAGPUR).

Generally known as Dr. Munje (or Moonje as he writes it himself). Born about 1875. Belongs to a Brahmin family of Poona. Educated at the Hislop College, Nagpur. In 1900 went to Bombay to study medicine; passed the test for Assistant Surgeons, and volunteered for the war in South Africa where he served till the end of the war. Thence he proceeded to England to study ophthalmology, and on his return to Nagpur about 1904 started practice as a doctor, making a speciality of eye cases. His father was a Government servant, and he has a brother Extra Assistant Commissioner in Berar, who was formerly professor in the Hislop College. Dr. Munje is said to be of good character, and to have a good social position in Nagpur.

In 1904 he started politics as a delegate to the Congress, and gradually became more and more extreme. In 1906 he accompanied Tilak and Khapardo to Calcutta when they went there to inaugurate the *Shivaji* celebration. Since then he has been the leading extremist in Nagpur. He appears to have been turned against Government by some matter connected with his service in South Africa in which he considers he was badly treated.

EASTERN BENGAL AND ASSAM.

NISHI KANTA BASU (OF BARISAL).

Born about 1872. Belongs to the Bakarganj District. Studied up to the middle vernacular class in his native village, and then in the homœpathic school at Dacca. Till 1905 he practised as a homœpathic doctor, and is generally known as Dr. Nishi Kanta Bose. After the anti-partition agitation started he was employed by the Bandhab Samiti (with which Aswini Kumar Dutt and Satish Chandra Chatterji, deportees, were connected) as an agitator on Rs. 25 a month. In spite of the deportation of his leaders he continued the agitation in 1909, and during that year was twice warned by the District Magistrate of the seditious nature of speeches delivered on 14th April at Barisal and on 8th October at Mymensingh ; since then Nishi Kanta has been less conspicuous.

SATISH CHANDRA CHATTERJEE (OF BARISAL).

Born about 1873. Of Bikrampur, Dacca. Educated at the Presidency College, Calcutta, and M. A. of Calcutta University.

Was Professor of Mathematics and Physical Science at the Brojo Mohan College, Barisal (see Aswini Kumar Dutt). Was Aswini Kumar Dutt's principal lieutenant in political organisation. Secretary of the *Bandhab Samiti* (declared an unlawful association in January 1909). As such the executive conduct of the agitation and of the volunteer movement was largely in his hands.

Deported in December 1908, as being the person most likely to carry on Aswini Kumar Dutt's work in his absence; otherwise of comparatively slight importance, although he is described as a person of much ability and of indefatigable energy. His deportation aroused no comment, as his case was completely overshadowed by that of his principal.

S. 05 Cr.

PULIN BEHARI DAS (OF DACCA).

Born about 1873 at Lonesingh, Faridpur, Eastern Bengal. Has some landed property in Tippera District. In 1908 an uncle of his was a Deputy Magistrate and another a *Munsif*, and a cousin Lal Behari Das, was Extra Assistant Commissioner of Sunamganj.

In September 1906 B. C. Pal and P. Mitter (Bar.-at-Law of Calcutta, recently deceased) visited Dacca and held meetings. P. Mitter asked those who were willing to sacrifice themselves for the country to stand forward and Pulin was one of those who did so.

Pulin shortly afterwards founded the Anusilan Samiti of Dacca, apparently following the advice of these two agitators. It had branches all over the province and was responsible for most of the political outrages committed since 1907 in Eastern Bengal. Pulin controlled the policy of the Anusilan Samiti; he was styled Captain General of Volunteers and under his leadership bands of volunteers armed with *lathis* used to drill and carry out mock fights, with the object first of resisting the police and afterwards of forming the nucleus of an anti-British rising throughout the province.

Pulin is an expert in *lathi*, sword, and dagger play, and besides instructing his volunteers himself used to send out trained volunteers to instruct the members of the subordinate *samitis*. As an organiser of political murders and crime he was the most dangerous man in the province, and under him the Anusilan Samiti of Dacca established a state of terrorism which has not yet subsided.

He was deported in December 1908, and thereafter an exhaustive enquiry into the Anusilan

Samiti and its branches was undertaken by the late Mr. Salkeld, I.C.S. Owing to his death the course of the enquiry was delayed, and on Pulin Behari Das's return from deportation in February 1910 he at once began to re-organise the Anusilan Samiti and to get into touch with his old associates. The case was at last completed and Pulin was re-arrested and is now the principal accused in what is known as the Dacca Conspiracy Case.

ASWINI KUMAR DUTT (OF BARISAL).

Born about 1850; of Batajore, Bakarganj District, Eastern Bengal. M. A., B. L. of Calcutta University. Zamindar with annual income of Rs. 6,000 to 8,000. Proprietor of the Brojo Mohan Institution (College and School), Barisal, and for some time Professor of English Literature and Law in this College. Member of the District Local Board where he was noted for his opposition to Government. Municipal Commissioner of Barisal from 17th March 1906 till his deportation. Well educated, good manners and of great local influence.

He began to agitate against the partition even before it took place, and in the autumn of 1905 Lord Curzon was burnt in effigy in the compound of his institution.

Throughout the following years he was the leader of the agitation in Eastern Bengal, and his institution was a centre of disaffection, almost all the processions and demonstrations in Barisal beginning or ending in the compound of his College. He took a prominent part in organising volunteers, and was president until his deportation of the Swadeshi Bandhab Samiti, which was declared to be an unlawful association under the new Act in January 1909. In order to gain the confidence of the people he did a good deal of charitable work through his Samiti and otherwise, and in the scarcity of 1906 he was able to collect Rs. 96,000 which were used in relieving the sufferings of the *Bhadralog* class (the class to which he himself belongs).

Aswini Kumar Dutt was so notoriously the leader of the agitation in Eastern Bengal that his deportation was recommended by the Local Government in July 1907 but negatived by the Government of India.

Attempts were made to deal with the local unrest in Bakarganj District by increasing the Police Force and applying the ordinary law, but this was found to be ineffectual. Aswini himself left Barisal for a time; he attended the National Congress at Surat in December 1907, and when it was broken up by the extremists under Tilak he took the side of the latter. Thereafter he toured in Bombay and the Central Provinces making speeches in the extremist interest and keeping in touch with B. G. Tilak of Poona and G. S. Khaparde of Amraoti. He returned to Barisal in July 1908 and renewed the Boycott agitation there. At an extremist meeting at Batajore in October 1908 a song was sung asking the audience "to gain their independence by the aid of the sword," but the singers were stopped by Aswini with the remark that "the time had not yet come for such songs."

He was deported in December 1908, and his case and that of K. K. Mitter were those which aroused the greatest amount of criticism in Bengal and throughout India. Attention was chiefly directed to the good work his "volunteers" had done in connection with famine and similar matters, and his extremist activities were denied or ignored.

On his return from deportation in February 1910 he excused himself from taking further part in politics on account of his age (about 60) and ill-health (he suffers from diabetes and Bright's disease). Since then he has taken very little part in agitation, and the Brojo Mohan Institution where the students were formerly taught, in the words of the District Magistrate, 'to hate everything British with a great and deadly hatred,' is being gradually brought round.

ANATH BANDHU GUHA (OF MYMENSINGH).

Born about 1851. Native of Tangail in Mymensingh District, of poor parentage. Is a B. A., B. L. of Calcutta University. On completing his education he returned to practice as a pleader at Mymensingh, where he soon became leader of the local bar and acquired a reputation as a pleader in criminal cases. Extremist pleaders are generally prominent in the defence of criminal cases, as such cases give them the best opportunity of embarrassing the magistrates and the Police. He has the local reputation of being unprincipled and unscrupulous, and there are several scandals about him. He is the leading political agitator in Mymensingh ; he is one of Surendranath Banerjea's channels of communication with Eastern Bengal and is frequently consulted by him as to the measures to be taken for keeping up the agitation.

In December 1908 proceedings were taken against Anath Bandhu Guha under section 108, C. P. C., and on December 18th he appeared before the District Magistrate and offered to give his bond in Rs. 10,000 with two sureties for his good behaviour for one year. This was accepted. He is still identified with the anti-partition agitation, but his activities now take a milder form.

AMBICA CHARAN MAZUMDAR (OF FARIDPUR).

Born about 1850. Belongs to the Faridpur District, Eastern Bengal. Educated at Barisal Zilla School and at the Metropolitan and Presidency Colleges, Calcutta. M. A., B. L. He is one of the leaders of the Faridpur bar and has a very extensive practice. Has an income from land of Rs. 1,500 to Rs. 2,000 a year. His social status is high and he is very influential in that part of the country.

Was a Congress-man, and after the partition became strongly anti-Government. At the end of 1907 he became more moderate in the expression of his political views. On January 3rd, 1908, after his return from the Surat Congress, he held a meeting at Faridpur at which he strongly condemned the conduct of Tilak and his party. He also seconded a resolution passed at this meeting sympathising with Mr. and Mrs. Allen in connection with the attempted assassination of the former at Goalundo the previous month. Ambica Babu presided this year (1910) over the Bengal Provincial Conference in September, and made a speech which was not free from objectionable features.

He poses as a moderate, but his speeches show that he is not anxious to smooth things down but rather to continue the unrest.

S. 05 Cr.

BHUPESH CHANDRA NAG (OF DACCA).

Son of the late S. C. Nag, Sub-Judge. Belongs to Barodi, Narainganj, Dacca, where he holds landed property jointly with his brother. The Nag family is very powerful in Barodi and the surrounding country. In 1908 Bhupesh had three cousins Sub-Judges, and one a Sub-Inspector of Police. A brother-in-law, J. C. Ghose, was a Deputy Magistrate.

In 1908 Bhupesh was just finishing his college career having passed the B. A. examination.

Bhupesh was second only to Pulin Behari Das in the Anusilan Samiti of Dacca. An expert in lathi-play, boxing and jiu-jitsu which he used to teach to the members of the Samiti.

As Pulin Das's most able lieutenant he was deported along with him in December 1908. After his release in February 1910 he remained for some time in Calcutta and afterwards returned to Dacca. His doings since then have been watched, and he seems to have withdrawn from open association with Pulin Behari Das. He is not one of the accused in the Dacca Conspiracy Case.

MADRAS.

V. O. CHIDAMBARAM PILLAI (OF MADRAS).

Born about 1873. Son of a private Vakil and petty landowner of Tinnevelly District. Educated at St. Francis Xavier's School, Tuticorin, and passed the Matriculation and pleadership examinations. Started practice as a pleader in 1896. In 1901 started a paper which shortly failed. In 1906 prominent in starting the Swadeshi Steam Navigation Company of Tuticorin. His dissolute habits are said to have alienated some local sympathy and capital from the Company.

From 1907 he was an agitator as well as a company promoter. At a meeting on 8th February 1908 he supported a resolution of sympathy with the families of Liakat Husain and Abdul Ghafur, recently convicted of sedition at Barisal. This was the beginning of his seditious campaign at Tuticorin where he delivered numerous speeches, along with a certain Subramania Siva, inciting the mill-hands to strike, and setting the people against the local Government officials. This went on till March 1908, and on the 13th of that month the unrest caused by these two agitators culminated in serious riots at Tinnevelly and Tuticorin.

In July 1908 Chidambaram Pillai was convicted of sedition in respect of his own speeches, and of abetment of sedition in respect of those delivered by Subramania Siva, and sentenced by Mr. Pinhey to transportation for life on both counts (the sentences to run concurrently). On appeal the sentences were reduced to 6 years' transportation.

K. G. PASUPATI AIYAR (OF MADRAS AND RANGOON).

Born about 1877. Son of a tax-collector of Karur Municipality (Madras). Educated at St. Joseph's College, Trichinopoly. Went to Rangoon in 1896. Was suspected of forgery as cashier of the Commercial Bank, but evidence for a prosecution was not obtainable. Made a large amount of money by speculation and manipulation of shares. His importance lies in his having financed V. V. S. Aiyar (now in Paris) and Madhav Rao (now in London), both important revolutionaries, and also T. S. S. Rajan (now in London) who was until the middle of 1909 also a prominent revolutionary, but has since withdrawn from active sedition. K. G. Pasupati Aiyar knows that the fact of his financing these seditionaries has been discovered, and has promised to discontinue supplies to the two first named.

S. 05 Cr.

G. SUBRAMANIA AIYAR (OF MADRAS).

Born about 1856. Brahmin of humble origin. Good education; B. A. of Madras University.

In 1883 started the *Hindu* Newspaper on Hindu Orthodox and anti-Christian lines; it was the expression of an anti-Christian Hindu revival which took place at that time in Madras. The paper afterwards developed into an anti-Government organ. Subramania Aiyar himself became in later years quite unorthodox and a social reformer; has crossed the seas (to England in 1897) and has married his widowed daughter to a man of a different sect.

In 1898 Subramania Aiyar gave up the *Hindu* but continued the *Swadesamitram,* a Tamil paper which he had been editing concurrently with the *Hindu* since 1883. It is the most influential vernacular paper in the Presidency; was very objectionable in 1907 and 1908 but has since become much milder in tone.

Many years ago he contracted a contagious disease on account of which the leaders of the Congress refused to give him any place of prominence. This is said to have done much to make him an extremist. He was in Madras, like Surendranath Banerjea in Calcutta, a great leader of the student community. His views, like those of his paper, have undergone a change in the last two years, and he is no longer so very prominent as an agitator, but he still goes as far as any of the Madras politicians.

VARAGANERI VENKATESA SUBRAMANIA AIYAR (NOW OF PARIS).

Generally known as V. V. S. Aiyar. Native of Trichinopoly, B.A. of Madras University. Practised for 2 years as a pleader at Trichinopoly. In 1907 went to Rangoon, and in 1908 went to England to study for the bar with the help of K. G. Pasupati Aiyar (*q.v.*).

V. V. S. Aiyar resided at the India House from July 1908 until before the Curzon-Wyllie murder (July 1909). He was Savarkar's right-hand man and an advocate of assassination. Took a great interest in discussing the possibility of sending arms to India, and bringing about an armed rising.

After Savarkar's arrest in March 1910 Aiyar became the leader; next month, learning how the secrets of the society had been given away in India by Chatturbhuj (formerly cook at the India House) and Koregaonkar of Gwalior he left for Paris, where he has since been, with Virendranath Chattopadhyaya, one of the leaders of the revolutionary party.

C. SUBRAMANIA BHARATI (OF PONDICHERRY).

Born about 1882. A Brahmin of the Tinnevelly District. Seems to have learnt his politics from G. Subramania Aiyar, as he was for a time a sub-editor of the *Swadesamitram*. In 1906 he edited a new English paper called the *Bala Bharat*. When this shortly failed he joined the staff of the seditious Tamil paper *India*. He resigned after two months and started the *Bala Bharat* again, which came to an end at last about July 1908. He joined the *India* again, and when the editor of this paper was arrested the same year he took refuge with the rest of the staff in Pondicherry. The paper continued to be published there, on more seditious lines than ever, for the next two years, but owing to the measures taken to prevent its import into British India it seems to have come to an end (1910).

Since Arabindo Ghose came to Pondicherry he has been a close associate of Subramania Bharati.

M. P. TIRUMALA CHARI *alias* TIRUMAL ACHARYA (OF MADRAS).

Born about 1887. Vaishnava Brahmin by caste. Cousin of S. Srinivasa Chari, and associate of C. Subramania Bharati in Pondicherry and one of the promoters of the seditious Tamil paper *India.*

This somewhat remarkable youth is known in London and Paris as Acharya. Before he left Madras, although a mere youth, he was known as a seditious character, and was registered printer and publisher of the *India* from August to November 1907. He was then replaced by Srinivasa Iyengar (convicted of sedition on the 13th November 1908 and sentenced to 5 years' transportation) but continued his connection with the paper. When the press was removed to Pondicherry on the arrest of the editor in July 1908, Acharya signed papers as proprietor of the *India* until he left for Europe in November 1908, when he handed over the management to his cousin S. Srinvasa Chari, with whom he has continued to correspond.

In London Acharya lived at the India House from January 1909 until the house was closed just before the Curzon-Wyllie murder (1st July 1909). It was reported at this time that Savarkar and others were urging him to become a 'martyr', and he appears to have leanings in that direction as he chose as an *alias,* when he attended the Egyptian National Congress at Brussels (September 1910), the name of Mr. Bhayankaram, which means the "terrific" or "awe-inspiring" one.

He is said to have copied out for the press most of the English version of Savarkar's book on the Mutiny.

In August 1909 he and Sukh Sagar Dutt (brother of Ullaskar Dutt, one of the bomb-makers of the

Maniktolla garden gang) started for Tangier to join the Riffs against the Spaniards and learn guerilla warfare. Dutt returned from Gibraltar, but Acharya got to Tangier where he was looked after for a month by a friendly Moor. He found it impossible to join the Riffs, and on V. V. S. Aiyar's instructions returned *viâ* Lisbon to Paris where he arrived in October.

He has not been to London since. A provisional warrant for his arrest under the Fugitive Offenders Act has been issued.

PUNJAB.

AJIT SINGH—(Last heard of at TEHRAN, PERSIA).

Born in 1879. Son of Arjan Singh, Jat Sikh by caste, originally of Jullundur City. Arjan Singh obtained a grant of two squares of land in the Chenab Colony and settled there as a cultivator.

Ajit Singh passed the Entrance Examination of the Punjab University and became an agent to Rai Bhagat Ram, Barrister of Jullundur. In 1895 Ajit Singh moved to Lahore, and made his living as a *munshi*, teaching Urdu and Punjabi to Europeans. His brother Kishen Singh was employed by the Arya Samaj as a clerk in the Hindu Orphanage, and on one occasion Ajit Singh was employed in his place to bring some Hindu orphans to Lahore as Kishen Singh was ill. The Arya Samajists, however, strenuously deny that Ajit Singh was a member of the Samaj, and describe him as an atheist.

In 1906 Ajit Singh was engaged by a Russian suspect named Lasseff as a munshi; except for this he had hardly come to notice at all before the beginning of 1907.

It is unnecessary to refer in detail to the seditious agitation set on foot by him at the beginning of 1907 which culminated in the Rawal Pindi riot of May 2nd. On the arrest of Lajpatrai on May 9th, Ajit Singh absconded, but was arrested in June at Amritsar and deported. He was released in November 1907 and returned to Lahore. He collected his old associates and started a campaign of flooding the Punjab with seditious literature in the form of books and pamphlets, mostly issued by the Bharat Mata Book Agency, in which he was encouraged and assisted by Amba Parshad and by his own brother Sowaran Singh who has since died (1910). Similar books, as part of the same scheme, were also prepared and issued by a person named Lal Chand Falak. When steps were taken to prosecute those responsible for this steady stream of sedition, Ajit Singh and Amba Parshad absconded before they could be arrested. They went to the Persian Gulf and after many wanderings were last heard of at Tehran. Ajit Singh in a recent letter said that he was anxious to return to India if the " misunderstanding of Government " could be removed, and accused Amba Parshad of having been his evil genius.

AMBA PARSHAD—(Last heard of at TEHRAN, PERSIA).

Born about 1865. Son of Govind Rai, Kayasth by caste, of Moradabad (U. P.).

Amba Parshad started as a school-master in Moradabad but was soon dismissed. Edited the Jami-ul-Ulum at Moradabad. Prosecuted for sedition in 1897 and absconded. Ultimately surrendered, and was sentenced on the 29th October 1897 to 18 months' rigorous imprisonment. In March 1899 re-started the Jami-ul-Ulum. In January 1901 he was prosecuted by the Minister of Rampur and by the Rani of Landhaura. He was convicted under the following sections of the Indian Penal Code, and awarded the sentences noted :—

(1) Section 500, Indian Penal Code (Defamation)—2 years' simple imprisonment.

(2) Section 500, Indian Penal Code—1 year's simple imprisonment.

(3) Section 506, Indian Penal Code (Intimidation)—Fined Rs. 1,000, or, in default, 6 months' simple imprisonment.

(4) Section 500, Indian Penal Code—2 years' simple imprisonment.

(5) Section 471, Indian Penal Code (Using as genuine a forged document)—2 years' rigorous imprisonment.

He was released from jail on the 10th of February 1907 and proceeded to Agra, where he stayed with the editor of the *Jasus*. He then went to Delhi and Lahore. In April he was offered the appointment of sub-editor of the *Hindustan*, and apparently at the time he accepted it, for his appointment as sub-editor was announced in the paper. He did not long retain this post, but joined the members of the Anjuman-i-

Mohibban-i-Watan, and became the editor of the society's organ, the *Bharat Mata*. The *Anjuman-i-Mohibban-i-Watan* (Society of lovers of their country) was the seditious society started in Lahore by Ajit Singh. In April 1907 Amba Parshad visited Gujranwala ; he was implicated in the publication of a seditious article in a paper called *India* of that place, and a warrant was issued but he absconded to Nepal. He was arrested by the Nepalese authorities and handed over in August 1907, and in December he was acquitted by the Sessions Judge, Lahore.

In 1908 he was associated with Ajit Singh in his seditious book agency, and absconded with him when proceedings were taken in 1909. He was last heard of along with Ajit Singh at Tehran.

RAM BHAJ DUTT CHAUDHARI (OF LAHORE).

Born about 1867. Son of Radha Kishen, Brahmin of the Gurdaspur District. Educated at the Forman Christian College, Lahore; B. A. of Punjab University; Pleader of the Chief Court, Lahore.

Ram Bhaj Dutt is a leader of the local Arya Samaj for which he has often worked as Secretary. In October 1905 married Sarala Devi (q.v.) who was already prominent in Nationalist circles in Calcutta. Thereafter Ram Bhaj Dutt became a more zealous politician.

Ram Bhaj Dutt was proprietor of the *Hindustan* newspaper, of which Amba Parsad (q.v.) was for a time sub-editor. The Press and the paper were purchased by him from Dina Nath and Ishri Parshad in July 1907, when Dina Nath was convicted of sedition. In July 1908 it was privately reported that both Ajit Singh and Amba Prasad were receiving pecuniary assistance from Ram Bhaj Dutt.

In August 1908 Ram Bhaj Dutt, then Secretary of the Arya Pratinidhi Sabha (the controlling body of the Arya Samaj for the Punjab) left for England. He did not do much there that was noticeable. He returned to Lahore in November 1908, and on 1st March 1909 he presented himself before Mr. Fenton, Chief Secretary to Government, saying that he contemplated applying for the vacant Governorship of Jammu, and inquiring whether, if the Maharajah referred to the Punjab Government the question of his loyalty, satisfactory assurances would be given on the point, as he had a misgiving that some of his speeches had been subject to misconception.

Since then he and his wife have been taking a loyalist line and mixing in European society. Ram

Bhaj Dutt of Lahore should not be confused with Pandit Bhoj Dutt Sharma of the *Masafir* of Agra.

SARALA DEVI (wife of Ram Bhaj Dutt). Born about 1882. Daughter of Mr. J. Ghosal of Calcutta, an old leader of the National Congress party. Has a brother Mr. J. Ghosal in the I. C. S. (Collector of Ratnagiri, Bombay 1910) who is married to the Princess Sukriti, daughter of the Maharajah of Cooch Behar.

Sarala Devi's mother was Secretary of the Ladies' Theosophical Society of Calcutta, and Babu Rabindranath Tagore, a well-known Bengali poet, is her uncle. Sarala Devi was not married at the customary early age, as her parents desired that she should devote her life to the service of the country. She was one of the originators of the Swadeshi movement in Calcutta long before the partition, and tried to rouse the people by reviving old festivals, starting music clubs for the cultivation of national songs, and setting up a kind of 'Hero-worship' by means of plays describing the doings of the Hindu heroes of the past. She was one of the first to start lathi-play and sword exercise in Bengal, and from 1902 to 1904 she had an athletic club where these exercises were taught at her father's house at Baliygunge. The teacher was a certain 'Professor' Murtaza. There can be no doubt that she was a thorough extremist, and that the object of all these movements was to rouse the national spirit and the national strength in Bengal, with a view eventually to driving the English out. The later agitation and disturbances in Bengal were simply the natural development of her work.

It has long been recognised in Bengal that no rising in India has any chance of success without the co-operation of the Punjab, which was the great stumbling-block to the mutineers in 1857. It is possible that Sarala Devi's marriage with Ram Bhaj Dutt of Lahore in October 1905 was arranged partly with a view to provide a link in the agitation between the two Provinces, and for a year or two afterwards there were indications that it was being used for this end. Lately, however, as has been noticed above, Ram Bhaj Dutt has begun to come round to the side of Government and Sarala Devi is apparently following the same course as her husband.

HAR DAYAL (OF DELHI).

Born about 1884. Son of the late Lala Gauri Dayal, Kayasth by caste, a reader in the District Court at Delhi.

Har Dayal had a brilliant academic career. Obtained the B. A. at Delhi, and at Lahore was first in the examination for the M. A. degree and was selected for a State Scholarship in England. In 1905 went to Oxford and joined St. John's College where he resided till 1907. He then resigned his Government scholarship, and although the College authorities were willing to continue his exhibition and even to procure him further assistance, he insisted on removing his name from the books. He then blossomed out as a complete nationalist who would accept no favours at the hand of Government or of any Englishman.

He was back in Lahore at the beginning of 1908, and in April of that year he and a party of youths he had collected stayed with Lajpatrai for a few days. He tried to impress his ideas on the Punjab extremists, but when he said that true Nationalism required that one should not help Government even by working as a pleader, this was too much for them (most of them being pleaders themselves) and even the *Panjabee* threw him over as a quixotic dreamer (*Panjabee*, August 5th, 1908).

Har Dayal left again for Europe in August 1908, and arrived in London in September. He then went to Oxford, whence he sent a number of enthusiastic but rather foolish letters to the Indian papers, chiefly the *Hindustan* and the *Panjabee* of Lahore.

In January 1909 he fell ill, and was ordered to take a complete rest for two months. He turned up next in Paris with Shyamji Krishnavarma, and in

June 1909 he was back in London, but shortly after went to Geneva where he edited the *Bande Mataram* with the financial assistance of Madame Cama. Towards the end of 1909 he returned to Paris, and in April 1910, he had to go to Algiers for his health (he suffers from consumption). He returned to Paris in July and went to stay with S. R. Rana (the Hindu merchant married to a German woman who finances the Paris revolutionary party).

Har Dayal has since (October 1910) left Paris for Marseilles. The real object of this journey is not yet known. He is by far the cleverest of the young extremists, but is quite unbalanced in his views and much handicapped by ill-health.

LALA LAJPAT RAI (OF LAHORE)

Born about 1862 (or 1865 according to another account); the son of Radha Kishen, Jain (Khatri) by caste of Jagraon in Ludhiana District. His father was employed by the Education Department as a Persian teacher; is now a pensioner of Government, and in 1907 kept a paper shop in Lahore.

Lajpatrai passed the Entrance Examination of the Punjab University but failed in the subsequent examinations. Became a pleader and started practice in Hissar in 1891, moving next year to Lahore. In 1897 he gave up most of his legal work and devoted himself to the Arya Samaj, by which he was employed as a preacher.

In 1905 Lajpatrai was selected by the Indian Association, Lahore, to represent the Punjàb on the Congress deputation then sent to England. From England he proceeded to America and returned to India in November 1905. Addressing a large meeting of 3,000 people on his arrival in Bombay he told them that memorials and petitions to Government had been of no avail, and the time had come when action should take the place of words.

During 1906 he toured and lectured in the Punjab, nominally on the *Swadeshi* movement. In October 1906 the *Panjabee* published a speech which he had intended to deliver at the Punjab Provincial Conference the previous month (it was not delivered as it was decided to conduct the proceedings in vernacular). In this he asked the Punjabees to make up their minds whether they " were ready for any sort of political activity" or should wait some time longer. He warned them that what he called 'real earnest political work' was not child's play, but a very risky and expensive game.

In December 1906 there was a demonstration in Sialkot against the enhancement of certain octroi rates. Lajpatrai was invited there, and on January 14th, 1907, he addressed a large meeting advising them not to yield to the threats of officials who were the servants of the people, and saying that it was an honour to go to jail for fighting for their rights.

In March he addressed at Lyallpur two meetings of protest against the Canal Colonisation Bill held by members of the Chenab Colony. He said foreigners could not rule unless the people were divided and disunited. They should unite for the honour of their forefathers who shed their blood to preserve their self-respect. Thousands died every day of plague; that was no glorious death. They should not fear jails or even death and their object would be achieved.

Lajpatrai was one of the proprietors of the *Panjabee*, and when the editor was prosecuted (and convicted) he defended him free of charge.

Early in April 1907 he delivered a speech at the Arya Samaj anniversary at Hissar which is said to have been of a seditious nature, and later in the month he paid a visit to Bombay with the object, it was rumoured, of consulting Tilak as to the state of affairs in the Punjab.

He returned to Lahore on May 1st and went on the same day to Rawalpindi where trouble was brewing as the result of the seditious activities of Ajit Singh. It was advertised in the *Panjabee* that Lajpatrai would preside at a mass meeting on the evening of May 2nd to protest against the Deputy Commissioner's order summoning certain pleaders to attend an enquiry in his court under the

Legal Practitioners Act for the support given by them to Ajit Singh. A riot, however, broke out on the morning of May 2nd and the proposed meeting was prohibited. Lajpatrai then returned to Lahore.

He was arrested on the morning of the 9th May 1907 and deported to Mandalay.

He was released in November 1907. His first public speech was made at the Arya Samaj anniversary in the grounds of the D. A. V. College, Lahore, on December 1st. He declared that he was willing to sever his connection with the Arya Samaj if his political activities had brought it into trouble. He concluded with a few words to the students of the college advising them not to go to the doors of others to beg but to stand on their own legs. "Take each other's hand, walk side by side, and then let us see what power in the world stands in our way."

In December 1907 he attended the Surat Congress and when it was broken up by Tilak and his followers, Lajpatrai openly sided with the Moderates.

In January 1908 he visited Calcutta, and meetings were held in his honour in Howrah Town Hall, and in College Square. At the latter Surendranath Banerjea presided and the Hon'ble Mr. Gokhale was also on the platform. The Calcutta visit seems to have reassured Lajpatrai and he began to become bolder again. (It was probably at this time that he decided to bring a civil suit against the *Englishman*, in which Mr. Justice Fletcher gave him substantial damages which were afterwards reduced on appeal.)

On his way back to Lahore he addressed meetings at Cawnpore and Delhi and had a great reception at both places. In February he visited Jullundur, Meerut, Aligarh, Agra and Muttra interesting himself in famine relief in the towns of the United Provinces. At one of his Agra meetings he said that the relief given by Government was really only money taken from the pockets of the people, and it was to be regretted that the people were not allowed to distribute it themselves.

In March and April he continued to interest himself in the famine in the United Provinces and sent out emissaries to work in the villages.

He was apparently disappointed at the state of affairs in Lahore, where political agitation was dying down, and in August 1908 he left for England. On his arrival in London he was driven to the India House, in which he had been one of the first residents when it was started in 1905. A private entertainment was held in his honour, but he did not stay there on this occasion, and on leaving he asked that nothing should be said about his visit.

During his stay in England he held aloof from the revolutionary party and tried to ingratiate himself with Members of Parliament in which he was fairly successful. He returned to India in March 1909.

The exposures in the case of Bhai Parmanand (q.v.) which Lajpatrai did his best to explain away, and differences among the leaders of the Arya Samaj on the subject of dissociating the Samaj from political agitation, somewhat damped Lajpatrai's public activity. Owing to the ill-health of his son Piari Kishen, Lajpatrai went to England to see him in 1910, and brought him back with him to Lahore in October. During his stay in England he did not associate with the extremists.

BHAI PARMANAND, M. A. (OF LAHORE).

Born about 1875. Native of the Jhelum District. Educated at the D. A. V. College (Arya Samaj), Lahore. Employed for many years as an itinerant lecturer and preacher of the Arya Samaj and later as a Professor at the D. A. V. College. Strong supporter of Lajpatrai and much under his influence.

In 1905 visited South Africa as an emissary of the Arya Samaj, and again a year or two later. In 1907 he was in England studying History at King's College, London. He returned in the cold weather of 1907-08 to Lahore, and was appointed Professor of History at the D. A. V. College, but he spent much of his time touring about the country in the interest of the Arya Samaj. In 1908 he visited the North-West Frontier Province, and toured in the Punjab and in Burma, and in 1909 he visited the United Provinces and toured in Madras.

In November 1909 several places were searched in Lahore in connection with the publication of seditious books by Ajit Singh and his party. Amongst them was the Bharat Mata Book Agency, on premises formerly occupied by Ajit Singh and Amba Parshad, and at the time of the search by Bhai Parmanand and Ajit Singh's two brothers, Sowaran Singh (since deceased) and Kishen Singh. In a box belonging to Professor Parmanand was found a copy of a manual on explosives and bombs similar to the one found in the Maniktolla garden, Calcutta, and the one found in the 'Savarkars' house at Nasik. There were other manuscripts relating to seditious and revolutionary schemes, and some old letters from Lajpatrai to Parmanand in England asking him to supply him with socialistic and revolutionary literature.

On the 18th April 1910 Parmanand was bound over for three years under section 110 (*f*), Criminal

Procedure Code, and an appeal against the order was rejected. On October 3rd, 1910, Bhai Parmanand left Bombay for Europe, giving out that he was going to study medicine.

On the discovery of the incriminating documents Parmanand was suspended by the D. A. V. College authorities, and, on the decision of the case, dismissed.

The genuineness of Lajpatrai's letters (in one of which Lajpatrai expressed fear lest the outbreak in the Punjab might be premature) was never contested, but Lajpatrai attempted in the press to explain away their obvious meaning. It is not clear why Parmanand should have kept such letters for over two years, but conspirators rarely trust each other and he may have kept them in order to have a hold over Lajpatrai.

UNITED PROVINCES.

BHOJ DUTT, SHARMA (OF AGRA).

Born about 1850. Son of a small landholder of the Muzaffarnagar District. Poor education. Led a wandering life for some years. Enlisted in the Dehra Dun police and rose to head-constable. In 1888 his services were dispensed with on suspicion of criminal misappropriation of property entrusted to him. He then drifted to the Punjab and was a *patwari* (revenue official) on Rs. 10 a month in Montgomery District. Here he became a Christian; this attracted the attention of the Arya Samaj who reconverted him, and he left Government service and became an Arya Samaj lecturer in 1898. In 1903 started, in Agra, the *Musafir* as an Arya Samaj journal. In this he made obscene attacks on other religions, and in June 1907 he was sentenced to 1 month's rigorous imprisonment under section 292, Indian Penal Code (obscenity), in respect of an article on the Mahomedan religion. In appeal the High Court commuted this to a fine of Rs. 500.

After this he calmed down for a time and took to attacking Government as a safer subject of criticism than religion. Gradually, however, the paper resumed its old courses of rabid writing against Mahomedans, and in 1910, Bhoj Butt was required to give heavy security under the Press Act, which he failed to furnish. The paper is for the present defunct, but may be continued by his son. As will be seen from his history he is a person of no importance who has brought himself forward purely by the extravagance of his writing on religious subjects. The suppression of his paper was received with delight by the Mahomedans and has not displeased the better class Hindus who consider that he brings his co-religionists into disgrace.

Pandiṭ Bhoj Dutt, Sharma, editor of the *Musafir* of Agra, should not be confused, as is frequently done, with Ram Bhaj Dutt Chaudhari, Chief Court pleader of Lahore, the husband of Sarala Devi.

MAHESH CHARAN SINHA (OF ALLHABAD).

Born about 1878. Kayasth by caste. Belongs originally to Lucknow. Educated at Lucknow and Allahabad ; B.A. of the Reid Christian College, Lucknow. Relative (nephew ?) of the Honourable Mr. Sachchidananda Sinha, Bar.-at-Law of Allahabad, editor of the *Hindustan Review*.

Mahesh Charan was sent in 1903 to Japan to learn engineering. He went on to America in 1904 and joined the Agricultural College, Corvallis, Oregon, United States of America. Obtained there the degree of M. Sc. in 1906, and high praise from the authorities. Did some research work in chemistry at the same Institution.

Early in 1907, he was in London, and was manager of the 'India House' for a time. In the *Indian Sociologist* for March 1907, he was reported to have delivered an "eloquent and powerful" speech at the annual meeting of the India Home Rule Society, presided over by Shyamji Krishnavarma. He returned to India about the middle of 1907 and tried unsuccessfully in several places to obtain employment as a teacher of chemistry or in some similar capacity. Stayed frequently from time to time with Sachchidananda Sinha at Allahabad.

In 1909 Mahesh Charan was made principal of the *Prem Mahavidyalya*, a National School at Bindraban, but he did not retain this employment long.

In 1910 he was engaged as teacher of chemistry at the Arya Samaj *Gurukul* near Hardwar, an institution of very doubtful loyalty.

While in America and in England Mahesh Charan Sinha was associated with several notorious extremists, and was regarded as a promising young revolutionary. Since his return to India his conduct has been occasionally suspicious but nothing has been proved against him.

S. 05 Cr.

HOTI LAL VARMA.

Born about 1877. Jat by caste. Of humble origin ; the son of a cultivator of the Muttra District. Educated at Agra Collegiate School and passed the Middle School Examination, but failed in the Entrance Examination of the University. After this said to have been converted by a Mr. Maclean, missionary, who sent him to St. Stephen's College, Delhi, to complete his education. Was there only a few months, and then went to calcutta where he was employed in the office of the *Amrita Bazar Patrika*.

His importance is that he links up many isolated phases of anarchist and revolutionary activity in India and abroad, and that the places and persons visited by him in his extended tour are all recorded by him in his diary.

In 1905-06 he wandered about India getting employment on various newspapers, the places visited being Agra, Ajmer, Bombay, Lahore, Muzuffarnagar, Meerut, etc., ending up in December 1906 again at the *Amrita Bazar Patrika* office in Calcutta.

He left Calcutta (December 1906) for Hong-Kong (arrived December 23rd, left 30th April 1907), Shanghai (arrived 3rd May), Kobe (arrived 4th June), Tientsin (arrived 27th June) and travelled in China till July 22nd, visiting the British Indian troops in China and attempting to create disaffection among them as he had done in Hong-Kong. On the 12th July he was turned out of the lines of the 41st Dogras.

He returned to India *viâ* Tuticorin (September 15th) and went to Pondicherry (16th). Here he stayed till October 3rd making friends and trying to arrange for the import of arms into India by this route. He then went to Bombay and was there from 6th to 14th November. He has recorded in his diary meetings during this time with 'Mr.

Tilak' and 'Mr. Khaparde' as well as with a Mr. R. K. Prabhu, who is believed to have been the Bombay Agent of the Maniktolla Garden conspirators.

On November 15th, 1907, he left for Europe, and arrived at Marseilles on December 5th. He sent a wire announcing his arrival to Shyamji Krishnavarma in Paris, and left the same night for Paris where he arrived next day. He stayed in Paris till December 22nd, and was seen off on the 23rd for London by Acharya (evidently the seditious young Madrassi M. P. Tirumala Chari) and Bapat (evidently P. M. Bapat of Ahmednagar, the Maratha bomb expert, for whom a warrant was issued in the Maniktolla case).

Hoti Lal stayed only three days in London and left again for India on December 27th *viâ* Marseilles (29th). He sailed on January 1st for Alexandria where he landed on the 6th and went to Cairo. There he interviewed Dr. Rutherford at the National Hotel and talked about 'Congress affairs'. From Cairo he went to Suez, and being hard up for money sent the following telegram of which the original has been recovered:— To Tilak, Poona. "Fifteen sterling required telegraphically." Varma.

It is not known whether the money was sent. He arrived in Karachi on January 31st, and after visiting one or two other places left Jodhpur on February 14th for Poona where he stayed with Mr. Tilak till the 25th. Here he met amongst others G. S. Chakravarti, manager of Arabindo Ghose's paper the *Bande Mataram* of Calcutta, and P. M. Bapat whom he had recently seen in Paris. He then went to Bombay (26th), where he met G. N. Potdar (B. A., Tokio), a Japan-returned suspect, and proceeded to Amraoti where he stayed with G. S. Khaparde from February 28th till March 2nd.

He then proceeded to Ahmednagar to look up P. M. Bapat, but failed to find him and went on to Madras where he stayed till March 10th. On this date he posted from Triplicane the seditious leaflet 'A message to the Punjabis' to Subedar-Major Ahmad Din at Hong-Kong, of which evidence was afterwards given at Hoti Lal's trial.

From 11th March to 9th April he was at Pondicherry, again making arrangements for the import of arms. He then went on to Calcutta (April 12th). Here he was associated with some members of the Maniktolla gang, and from some notes in his diary and from other evidence it appears that he visited the lines of the 10th Jats (he is a Jat himself) at Alipore, ostensibly for subscriptions. He then went on to Ranchi, Allahabad and Aligarh (arrived 21st April).

On 11th May he sent a telegram to the *Bande Mataram* of Calcutta, which was published in the issue of May 13th, as 'from our special correspondent,' in which he expressed sympathy with the Maniktolla anarchists under trial and with the assassins of Muzaffarpur.

Meanwhile the leaflet 'A message to the Punjabis' appeared in Aligarh, and evidence of the delivery of seditious speeches by Hoti Lal was also collected. He left Aligarh on May 19th for Agra and was arrested in the Jat boarding house there on May 25th. He was convicted on 28th July 1908 and sentenced to 7 years' transportation. He was subsequently tried in a supplementary case under section 124-A, I. P. C., for disseminating the seditious leaflet mentioned above, and for preaching sedition on various occasions, and sentenced on 1st October 1908 to 5 years' rigorous imprisonment on each of three charges, the sentences to run concurrently. On appeal to the High Court the sentence of seven years' transportation was reduced to 5 years' transportation and the sentence of 5 years' rigorous imprisonment was converted to 5 years' transportation, the sentences to run concurrently.

G. M. Press, Simla,—No. S. 05 Cr;—17-11-10.—30.—H.A.W.

INDEX.

A

B

C

M

N

P

R

S

T

U

V